Nathan Lewis Rice

The Pulpit: It's Relations to Our National Crisis

A Sermon preached in Fifth Avenue and Nineteenth Street Presbyterian

Church

Nathan Lewis Rice

The Pulpit: It's Relations to Our National Crisis
A Sermon preached in Fifth Avenue and Nineteenth Street Presbyterian Church

ISBN/EAN: 9783744754231

Printed in Europe, USA, Canada, Australia, Japan

Cover: Foto ©Lupo / pixelio.de

More available books at **www.hansebooks.com**

THE PULPIT: ▬

ITS

RELATIONS TO OUR NATIONAL CRISIS.

A SERMON,

PREACHED IN FIFTH AVENUE AND NINETEENTH
STREET PRESBYTERIAN CHURCH.

BY

N. L. RICE, D.D.

NEW YORK:

CHARLES SCRIBNER, 124 GRAND STREET.

1862.

THE PULPIT:

ITS RELATIONS TO OUR NATIONAL CRISIS.

---•••---

Then said he unto them, Render therefore unto Cæsar the things
that are Cæsar's, and unto God the things that are God's.—
MATT. XXII. 21.

THE efforts of bad men to injure the cause. of
religion, and to gain for themselves a cheap popularity by destroying the influence of its faithful
teachers, has given occasion to the utterance and
the defence of some of the most important and
precious truths of divine revelation. Thus, the
attempt of the Pharisees to entangle our Lord in
his talk, and in this way to convict him of disloyalty to Cæsar's government, led to the incul-
cation of one of those great principles of religion
which is to control the conduct of his people to
the end of time, namely, Fidelity to God, first
and chiefly ; and fidelity, secondly, to the civil

governments under which his providence may place them. Paul's defences of himself against the slanders of his enemies, contain truths of so much value, that they were placed on record for the instruction of the Church in all future time; and the false accusations against the followers of Christ, in the early ages of Christianity, called forth those Apologies for the Christian Religion, which accomplished so much for the cause of truth. Thus in every age God has made the wrath of man to praise him, by overruling the slanders heaped upon his servants, for the furtherance of the Gospel. Paul, whilst a prisoner at Rome, wrote to the church at Philippi, saying: "But I would ye should understand, brethren, that the things which happened unto me have fallen out rather to the furtherance of the Gospel." And the imprisonment of Baxter and Bunyan resulted in the writing of books which have proved a thousand times more efficacious than their public preaching, in the diffusion of the doctrines of the Gospel.

It need not, then, be regretted, that slanders published in this city and in other places, have made it proper for me to depart, on the present occasion, from my ordinary course, and to speak on subjects which I seldom deem it expedient to introduce into the pulpit, namely, *The state of the country, and my own position with reference to it.* I do this in accordance with the advice of judicious friends, and with the design immediately to publish the discourse.

1. I pursue this course, not for the purpose of stirring up the patriotic feeling of my people. There is not the slightest necessity for this. Their conduct is the conclusive evidence that their love of their country is sufficiently intense. Indeed, it would be little to the credit of any Christian congregation, to admit their need of exhortation on such a subject, in such a day as this.

It is important, however, to remark, that patriotism is not, as many seem to imagine, a Christian virtue. It is, like natural affection, the spontaneous feeling of the heart. It is as natural for me to love my country as to love my home; and as there are multitudes of men, not Christians, who tenderly love their firesides and their families, so are there multitudes of true patriots, who do not profess to be Christians. Indeed, it not unfrequently happens in both cases, that that which is natural to the mind becomes too strong. How often are fathers and mothers chargeable with a species of idolatry in the affection which they lavish on their children—

giving them a place in their hearts which is due only to God. And so do men not unfrequently love their country so intensely, as to forget or disregard the rights of other nations ; and Christians, in their intense devotion to their country, in its struggles, constantly lose sight of the interests of the Church of Christ, which, in our day, is in no less peril.

It is, nevertheless, true, that Christianity exerts a most important influence on both natural affection and patriotic feeling—elevating both, and giving them a wise direction. It moderates the love of country, when it would become too exclusive, and makes men *philanthropists* as well as patriots ; and it teaches them how to advance the true interests both of their own country and of mankind.

Have you ever observed, that there is in the Bible no command to love one's country ? You find no such precept in the Decalogue, nor is there any such in the Gospel ; nor is patriotism ever placed in any enumeration of the Christian virtues, any more than is natural affection. If a minister of the Gospel were about to preach on this subject, he might be perplexed to find a text. We do, indeed, find commands to obey the powers that be, to pray for civil rulers, and the like; but all this is required of one even temporarily sojourning in any country. Now, since the Bible is a perfect rule of duty, as well as of faith, why do we find in it no command or exhortation to love our country? Not because patriotism is not most important, but because it is *natural*, just as it is natural for members of the same family to love each other. If a father have ceased to love his children, it is because depravity has destroyed natural affection. How can the affection thus destroyed be restored? Not merely or chiefly by exhorting him to love his family. The control of evil passions over his mind must be broken; and then natural affection will resume its sway. Purify and elevate his moral feelings; and then, and not till then, will he again love his family, and cherish the children whom he had abandoned or abused. And so, if a man have ceased to love his country, it is because this noble affection, so natural to the mind, has been smothered by selfishness and degrading passions. It is vain to preach to such a man the duty of loving his country. The reign of depravity in his heart must be subdued, and then he will again cherish the country of his birth, or of his adoption.

We cannot but admire the divine wisdom in

1*

this thing. God has not commanded us to love our country, but he has inculcated those moral principles which elevate and wisely direct that love of country, which is natural. It has always seemed to me, therefore, that for Christian ministers to spend any considerable time in preaching patriotism is quite unnecessary, if indeed in so doing they are not travelling beyond the inspired record. If men become Christians, they will surely be patriots. Nay, unless depraved dispositions have gained a fearful sway, the love of country, naturally strong, must exist; and if depravity has overcome it, that depravity itself must be overcome. There is, consequently, no way in which ministers of Christ can do so much to promote patriotism, as by preaching the Gospel in its purity; for then they bring to bear on the mind of man an influence which gives to that which is natural its full sway, and secures to it a wise direction.

Still less is it necessary or proper for ministers to preach patriotism to their people, at a time when with all but the most depraved, the love of country is intensely aroused; or to declaim in favor of war, when the whole country is in a blaze of excitement. Ministers are called by their people to instruct them in those truths of Divine revelation, which they are supposed to understand somewhat better than they; to stimulate and guide those Christian virtues, which are always too feeble, and are constantly liable to decay; and to turn men from sin to God. So far as our country is concerned, there are two classes of principles and of feelings, which are essential to its peace and prosperity: patriotism and sound morals. Now, is it not true, that so far as the latter is successfully cultivated, the former is sure to be strong enough? And has it not been our boast, that the troubles of our country, in the very beginning of them, called forth such a burst of patriotic feeling, as we never before witnessed? I entered upon my labors amongst you in the midst of the prevailing excitement; and no one could imagine, for a moment, that it needed to be intensified. In the name of reason, why should ministers of Christ labor to increase that class of feeling, already excited to the intensest pitch, instead of employing their time and their energies to strengthen those religious and moral affections admitted to be far too weak, and in danger of becoming still more feeble, whilst other feelings are so intensified? Is he a wise and faithful watchman, whose voice is heard shouting, where there

is confessedly no danger, instead of guarding the
exposed parts of the city ?

2. Again, I do not discuss the subject already
announced, for the purpose of satisfying my own
people that the charge of sympathizing with *Secession*, published by certain newspapers, is false
and slanderous. They know, that one of the first
duties I performed, when I entered upon my
labors amongst them, was to meet with and address the ladies of my church, about to organize
themselves into a society to prepare bandages and
other necessaries for wounded soldiers. They
have heard me, fifty times over, pray for the
destruction of secession. They have heard me,
Sabbath after Sabbath, pray for the President of
the United States and his counsellors, for Congress,
and for all in authority, that God would direct
them to such measures as He could approve, and
to bless those measures to the restoring of the
Constitution and the laws over our whole country ; that we might again have one united country, as in days past. Now, allow me to propose
two questions :

1st. Would it be possible for any but a con-
summate hypocrite, to offer such prayers, if he
desired the success and permanency of the Southern Confederacy ? Do you see how one, sym-

pathizing with secession, could pray that God would direct our government to the use of means by which the Union would be restored?

2d. If these prayers should be answered, would we not have all that we profess to be struggling for? Does any true friend of the country desire any thing more than this? And is there any true Christian, who is unwilling to leave it to the infinitely wise God, in whose hands are the hearts of all men, to determine in what way and by what means our Union shall be restored? I do not wonder that my prayers do not suit those whose aim is not the restoration of the Union under the Constitution, but the abolition of slavery at whatever cost; who did so much to bring the war on the country, and have done so much to cripple the Government ever since its commencement. I saw, the other day, in a religious newspaper, the same charge made against the President's pastor; though I have not learned that the President himself has found any fault.

This vindication is not necessary to satisfy my own people; for from them I have received nothing but kindness, since I accepted their call and commenced my labors amongst them. Indeed it is due to them to say, that their generosity has been of an extraordinary character.

3. I have three reasons for departing, to-day, from my ordinary course of pulpit instruction :

1st. I do it, because it is not right for a Christian minister to suffer his usefulness to be impaired, or the ministry to be reproached, by allowing slanderous publications to pass unexposed. For such reasons the apostle Paul found it necessary, more than once, to defend himself against such attacks. I am not so ignorant of human nature, as to expect to silence such men. This cannot be done, especially at such a time as the present. Our Lord did, for the time, silence those who sought to convict him of disloyalty ; yet when he was tried for his life, they were not ashamed to testify : " We found this fellow perverting the nation, and forbidding to give tribute to Cæsar." But whilst such men will still repeat their falsehoods, there are multitudes of fair-minded and reasonable men, who will be satisfied.

In times of great excitement, whether the excitement be of a religious or a political character, those public men, who keep cool, who are accustomed to examine principles, and to observe results, and who foresee evils that must inevitably follow the operation of false principles, may think themselves happy, if they suffer nothing worse than slander. In the beginning of this century, an extraordinary revival of religion prevailed in the West, and especially in Kentucky, my native State. In its earlier stages, great numbers were converted ; but in the progress of things, the excitement degenerated into the wildest fanaticism. Then began that curious phenomenon called *the jerks ;* and in the end, some even of the ministers united with that singularly fanatical sect, called *Shakers ;* and others formed a new Unitarian sect. Then those ministers who saw the danger, and lifted the warning voice, amongst whom was a venerable kinsman of my own, were bitterly denounced by other ministers and by the people, as enemies of the revival—as opposers of the work of God ; and for a length of time, great odium rested on them, until the deplorable fruits of the fanaticism vindicated their wisdom and their fidelity. A similar state of things prevailed in some of the more eastern States, within the last thirty years. Crowds followed certain *revival preachers ;* and converts were counted by scores and hundreds. Then again faithful ministers, who dared to oppose the fanaticism, or even to stand aloof from it, were pronounced unregenerate, and were denounced as enemies of revivals. The fruits of those revivals soon vindicated them ;

and the region of country over which they spread, was familiarly called *the burnt district.*

Civil and political excitements operate in the same way, especially in time of war. For two years, the prophet Jeremiah pined in prison, part of the time in a loathsome dungeon, under the charge of *treason.* The evidence that he *sympathized* with the invading foe, was found in the fidelity with which he warned the king, the princes, the priests, and the people, that the only hope of saving the holy city and the nation from ruin, was in immediate repentance and reformation ; and none were found more bitter against him, than the false prophets and the corrupt priests. And because they made loud professions of patriotism, and prophesied of certain victories, they were held in honor, whilst the one true patriot in the city, was ignominiously beaten and imprisoned. In such times, those men are most popular, who assert what the people desire to hear, not those who dare to give warnings that might save them from ruin.

None of us have forgotten how the venerable commander of our army was assailed, soon after the commencement of the present unhappy war, as at heart a traitor, pretending to seek the overthrow of the rebellion, yet secretly intending no such thing ; as a sympathizer with secession ; nor have we forgotten from what quarter these insinuations came. When a man, who has won for himself a world-wide fame, as one of the most patriotic and skilful generals, by fighting his country's battles, can be assailed, at four-score years of age, with such charges ; who can expect to escape? And although terrible disasters, consequent upon these attacks, filling the land with alarm and mourning, for a time silenced the clamors and injurious accusations of such men ; it is to be apprehended that the same spirit is yet at work, and may bring upon the country other disasters.

2d. It is due to my people, as well as to myself and my office, that I should make public my views on this subject. It is not right for me to allow them to be held up before the public, as having a pastor who is false to his country. I propose, therefore, to put into their hands the means of refuting the slander.

3d. I pursue the course just indicated, still further, for the purpose of presenting some great truths, which may serve to guard the church against dangers which now threaten it, as well as the country.

If, in what I have to say, I shall depart from

my uniform habit by speaking of myself, the circumstances will be admitted as a sufficient ex-
cuse.   It is always painful to me to speak of myself in the pulpit; and you will bear me witness,
that I have uniformly avoided it.

What I propose to say, will be in answer to
the following question, suggested by the text,
viz. : *What do we owe to God and our country in
such a day as this?*

1. We owe it to God and our country, to hold
and to proclaim the Gospel in its purity. Nothing else can save the souls of men from sin; and
nothing else can save the country from the perils
that so thickly environ it. We must hold and
proclaim the *doctrines* of the Gospel, as well as
its precepts and its promises, unadulterated by
human philosophy. There has always been
amongst men a demand, on one ground or another, for something different; for the Gospel
" is not after man." So far from it, that Paul
said, " If I yet pleased men, I should not be the
servant of Christ." " The Jews," said he, " require a sign, and the Greeks seek after wisdom ;
but we preach Christ crucified, to the Jews a
stumbling block, to the Greeks foolishness; but
to them that are called, both Jews and Greeks,
Christ, the power of God and the wisdom of God."

Neither Jews nor Greeks were disposed to accept that which alone the apostle had to give. The one demanded a sign from heaven, the other insisted upon abstruse philosophic speculations. The apostle did not seek to gratify either of them. If we would save men we must not give them what they may demand, but what they need—the pure Gospel of the Son of God.

And as nothing but the Gospel can save the soul, so, as just remarked, nothing else can save the country. There are three powers, one or the other of which must control in civil society, viz. : *brute force*, as in despotisms ; *interest and passion*, as in anarchy ; *moral principle*, as in free governments. The Gospel only can sustain that moral principle, which is essential to the permanency of a free government. " I am inclined to think," said De Tocqueville, " that if faith be wanting, he must serve ; and if he be free, he must believe." A far higher authority has said : " Blessed is the nation whose God is the Lord." It is certain, that every one truly converted and rightly instructed, will be a true patriot.

What are the perils that now threaten our country ? Not the war now raging, fearful as it surely is. I never have believed that our chief danger lay in that direction. There are two dangers which are more to be dreaded, than all others, viz. : *immorality* and *fanaticism*—a lack of faith and disregard of God's law, on the one hand, and a perverted faith and false principles of moral reform, on the other. But for the prevalence of these two evils, the war never would have come upon the country ; and but for the prevalence of these, during the last year, the war might have had a favorable termination, ere this time. There are times, when error takes the form of cold, philosophic speculation ; but in an age of prevailing excitement it assumes the form of fanaticism. In the first-mentioned form, it has no power, but leaves the passions of men uncontrolled ; in the second, it gives to depravity a religious direction. And there is no phase of human corruption more destructive of the interests of Church and State, than fanaticism.

A few Sabbaths since, I had occasion to read to you an extract of a letter from the late venerable Dr. Alexander, of Princeton, written twenty-five years ago to a missionary in Ceylon, for the purpose of showing that men who observe the working of moral principles, can see further into the future, than those whose attention is mainly occupied with principles of a different character. He, at that time, distinctly foresaw the crisis that is now upon us.*

Let me now state another opinion expressed by the same eminent minister of Christ., viz. : that this country seemed destined to be overrun with all manner of fanaticism. Events thus far have but too fully verified the opinion ; and there is reason to fear, that we have seen but the beginning of the evil. Now there is nothing but the Gospel that can secure a pure morality ; and nothing else can restrain fanaticism.

In accordance with these views, my first sermon, on coming amongst you, was on the language of Paul to the church at Corinth : "And I, brethren, when I came to you, came not with

* The following is the extract above referred to : "As you see the New York papers, there is no occasion for me to say any thing of the public concerns of Church or State. I may observe, however, that we are in a very unsettled condition. The prosperity of the United States has been unprecedented now for half a century, and there is nothing to hinder its continuance and increase but the folly and wickedness of the people; but there are many indications in the manifest signs of the times, that we, as a nation, are rapidly approaching a crisis. The subject of slavery has been so imprudently managed, that a spirit of hostility between the northern and southern States has been excited, which in my opinion will not cease until a rupture shall take place, which will mark the end of our prosperity." This letter was written June 10th, 1836.

excellency of speech or of wisdom, declaring unto you the testimony of God. For I determined not to know any thing among you, save Jesus Christ and him crucified." The Christian minister goes forth under a commission, authorizing and requiring him to declare to men " the testimony of God," the great central truth of which, and that which gives value to all the rest, is *Christ crucified.* On matters respecting which God has borne no testimony, his ministers have no message, and can deliver none. From the ground then taken, I can never depart, as I expect soon to give account to God, before whom I stand.

A sermon was preached, a few months since, by one of the most venerable and prominent ministers of New England, which should have a wide circulation. I refer to the Rev. Dr. Hawes, of Hartford, Conn. The sermon was preached at an ordination in New Haven. The title of it is : " *The decay of power in the Pulpit.*" The very title, at such a time as this, is alarming ; for you know, my brethren, that the decay of power in the pulpit means the decay of religion in the churches, and of sound morals in the country. The preacher not only admits, but affirms the fact, that the decay has taken place.

What is the cause of this decay ? I quote his

own language. The chief cause, as he states it,
is, "*Dropping from its inculcations the great,
distinguishing doctrines of grace.*" Now, how
does it happen that these doctrines are so exten-
sively dropped? Says he, "The demand is for
something more exciting, more entertaining and
tasteful; and the modern pulpit is too much inclined to fall in with this demand, to discuss literary and ethical questions, questions of social and
moral reform, or other matters of a curious and
novel character, instead of bringing forward and
giving prominency to the old, and as some would
say, worn-out doctrines of depravity, regenera-
tion, sovereignty, election, justification, together
with the character and work of a crucified, aton-
ing Christ, as the great central point of all Gospel truth. It is rather rare," he adds, "that the
people hear a thorough-going, out-and-out discussion and application " of these and other kindred
doctrines.

The source whence this testimony comes, gives
it importance. Dr. Hawes is at the greatest remove from a tendency to extreme views on the
subject concerning which he speaks; yet he is con-
strained to testify, not only that the great doctrines
of the Gospel have, to a great extent, disappeared
from the pulpit, but that it has become common for

ministers of the Gospel to travel beyond the limits of their commission in search of novel, exciting, popular themes. "Instead," he remarks,
" of coming right out in the strength of God, with
the naked sword of the Spirit to do battle with
sin and error, it is too common for the preaching
of our day to study to be ingenious, original, elegant; to make literary sermons, great sermons,
popular sermons, as one says. To this end, instead of confining itself within its proper commission, that of delivering God's message in God's
way, it ranges abroad over creation to find novel
and strange subjects; and then it seeks to handle
them in a new and original way; decking them
out in tropes and figures, and all fine things, just
suited to make the whole exhibition elegant and
popular, it may be, but utterly ineffective and
powerless as to all spiritual impression." The
plain English of all this is, that, to a great extent,
the ministers of Christ have ceased to seek to form
the principles and mould the characters of their
hearers by the power of God's truth and Spirit,
and have begun to travel beyond the limits of
their commission to cater to a vitiated public
taste, and to gain popularity. In 1856, whilst
spending a few weeks in New England, I published statements respecting the state and tenden-

cies of the pulpit, precisely in accordance with the testimony now borne by Dr. Hawes. Those statements gave grave offence, and their correctness was boldly denied by one of the papers in Boston. Since that time, the tendencies have been rapidly downward, not only in New England, but very generally through the country; and within the last twelve months, the broad line between secular and religious themes has been almost obliterated. No wonder, then, that there has been a sad decay of power in the pulpit; and a sad decline in religion and morals.

In one of the discourses I had occasion to deliver in this church, just before the national Fast, I took occasion to state the limits within which, according to the Scriptures, the functions of the ministerial office are to be exercised. There are two classes of questions, as I stated, which ministers as such, are not authorized to discuss or determine, viz. : questions purely secular, civil, and political; and those moral questions which depend upon these. I did not say, as several reviewers represented me, that ministers cannot properly discuss and determine moral questions *connected with* secular, civil, and political questions, but moral questions which *depend upon* secular, civil, and political questions. As I then

2

stated, the Church and the State " are obliged, to
a considerable extent, to deal with the same subjects ; " that " to a considerable extent, criminal
legislation and ecclesiastical discipline take cog-
nizance of the same actions ; and then marriage,
the Sabbath, &c., have both civil and religious
aspects." In relation to all those subjects, which
have both of these aspects, the State legislates
purely with reference to the civil, the Church
exclusively with reference to the moral and religious. Thus, in relation to these two aspects of
marriage, Blackstone says : " Our law considers
marriage in no other light than as a civil con-
tract. The *holiness* of the matrimonial state is
left entirely to the ecclesiastical law ; the tem-
poral courts having no jurisdiction to consider
unlawful marriage as a sin, but merely as a civil
inconvenience."

I cannot better explain my position on this
subject, than by quoting from an article on the
Pulpit and the Press, which I published some
seven years ago : " What is the duty of ministers
of Christ in relation to political questions which
involve moral principles ? Undoubtedly there are
such questions. Suppose, for example, it were
proposed, as it has been, to abolish the Sabbath
laws or to abolish capital punishment ; in such

case, undoubtedly, the Christian ministers would have a duty to perform. If faithful, they could do no less, than carefully instruct their people and the civil rulers out of the word of God, and urge them to discharge their duty. *Such* interference with politics no reasonable man could object to. So in regard to slavery, most certainly, it is the duty of ministers of the Gospel fully and faithfully to expound in the hearing of their people the whole of the language of the Scriptures in reference to it, and teach them out of the Scriptures their precise duty." In a word, since Christ's ministers are commissioned to "declare the whole counsel of God," wherever he has legislated, they are bound to speak, whether it be to teach those great principles of his word by which civil rulers are bound to govern their official conduct; or to instruct individuals respecting their duties in the different relations of life.

But there are questions purely secular, civil, and political, respecting which God has not legislated. There are, as Blackstone says, "a great number of indifferent points, in which both the Divine law and the natural leave a man at his own liberty; but which are found necessary for the benefit of society to be restrained within certain limits. And herein it is that human laws have their greatest force and efficacy ; for with regard to such points as are not indifferent, human laws are only declaratory of, and act in subordination to the former (the Divine)." Now, since in relation to these purely secular and civil questions, God has given no revelation and has left men at liberty ; his ministers, as expounders of His revelation, have no right, as ministers, to say a word.

But there are innumerable moral questions which arise in connection with such secular questions, the decision of which must depend absolutely upon the decision of the secular questions. Let me illustrate. A physician is attending upon a patient with a diseased limb ; and ultimately the question comes up, whether he ought to resort to amputation. This is a strictly moral question ; for the life of the patient depends upon it. Shall he go to his pastor,.and ask him, as his instructor in religion and morals, to decide this question for him ? Shall he call a meeting of Presbytery, that by the united wisdom of its theologians the question may be safely determined ? Why not ? The question is strictly a moral one ; and it is of great importance. The answer is obvious. The moral question *depends upon* the scientific, and so soon as the latter is determined, the former is clear. What could any minister or any number of ministers say, were such a question submitted to them? They could say only, that if the case can be so treated, as to save both life and limb, it is wrong to amputate; but if amputation is necessary to the saving of the patient's life, it is duty to amputate. And they could say, that the physician is morally bound to use all his skill, and avail himself of all the means within his reach to determine, whether amputation is necessary to the saving of the patient's life. But all this would throw no light on the question pressing his conscience, whether he ought, or ought not to resort to amputation. Who can aid him in settling this question? Only scientific physicians. This is an example of a moral question *depending upon* a secular question; and ten thousand questions of the kind are constantly arising in medical practice.

Take another example. The President of the United States, at his inauguration, bound himself by a solemn oath to uphold the Constitution. Soon after, the question came up for decision, whether he should suspend the right of *Habeas Corpus*. Was it morally right for him to do this? Suppose he had called on his pastor, as his teacher on moral and religious subjects, to aid him in deciding the question ; what could his pastor have said ? He could have said, " If the Constitution gives you the power to suspend the right of *Habeas Corpus ;* and if the state of things is such as to demand the exercise of this extraordinary power, then it is right to do it." But this would be saying nothing but what every one knows. The President did not apply to his pastor, but to the Attorney-General ; for in this case the moral question depended wholly upon the civil. Since his pastor, though an able theologian, was not authorized or qualified to expound the Constitution, he could afford him no aid.

Again : Let us suppose that the late difficulty between the United States and Great Britain had resulted in a war, as it would, if certain individuals had not been delivered up to the latter ; then there would have been a very important question respecting the righteousness of the war, on the one side, and on the other. Suppose this question had been brought before the General Assembly of the Presbyterian Church, as a body authorized to teach morals and religion ; how could that body have given any decision whatever ? It would be easy to say, that if in taking those persons from an English vessel, and refusing to give them up, the United States violated the law of nations, the war on our part would be morally wrong; but if there was no violation of the law of nations, then the war on the part of England would be morally wrong. But all this would leave the question of the righteousness of the war undecided. How could the Assembly decide it? Since the right or wrong would depend upon the correct interpretation of the law of nations, the only way in which such a body could decide such a moral question, would be by setting its members to studying international law. And when we remember how confused and contradictory were the deliverances of lawyers and statesmen on the subject, we need be at no loss to judge how successful a body of ministers and elders would be in the investigation. But can any thing be more absurd, than to require or permit those whose office confines them to the study and exposition of the Scriptures, to discuss and determine questions depending upon secular, civil, and political questions, which it is no part of their business to study?

In relation to all such questions, the Christian minister stands to those whom it is his business to instruct, very much as a judge stands related to a jury. The duty of the judge is to expound the law; the business of the jury is to apply the law, as expounded, to the case in hand, and thus determine the guilt or innocence of the party on trial, or the right and wrong, as the case may be. The judge hears the whole of the testimony, and doubtless forms his opinion, and there may not be a man on the jury so capable of forming a correct opinion. But he may not express his opinion. He can only expound the law to the jury, and then say to them, "If from the testimony you believe thus and so, you will find for the plaintiff; but if you believe thus and so, you will find for the defendant." He may solemnly charge them to weigh the testimony impartially, and seek to come to a just conclusion. Precisely so stands the minister of Christ to those moral questions, which depend upon secular or civil questions. He can teach and impress upon men the principles of God's word; but, in all such cases, they must make the application. He cannot teach the physician what treatment he ought to adopt, that he may restore the health of a patient; but he can inculcate the solemn duty of using all the means within his reach to learn how to treat every case, and to be faithful in his efforts to effect a cure. He cannot teach the statesman what course he ought to pursue in relation to the questions that arise from time to time; but he can teach him those general principles of God's word by which civil officers are bound to govern their conduct, and his obligation to acquaint himself fully with the duties of his office, and to aim to secure the best interests of his country. He cannot tell the men in his church for which of two candidates, holding different political opinions, they ought to vote; but he can teach them their obligation to inform themselves, and cast their votes conscientiously for the best interests of the country. He cannot tell the merchant how to conduct his business; but he can teach the moral principles which are to control all business transactions, and exhort him to be "diligent in business." Thus the Christian minister, without knowing any thing of the science of medicine, may exert a powerful influence to make the most faithful and skilful physicians. Without understanding civil law, he may exert a mighty influence in making the best lawyers and statesmen. Without understanding the details of secular business, he may exert an influence to make the best business men. Thus the influence of the Christian ministry may be all-pervading, and most happy, whilst ministers stand aloof from secular matters, and confine themselves to the teaching of that noblest of all sciences, which is sufficient to tax the powers of an angel.

In a word, the inspired writers taught men in two ways. They inculcated those duties which are everywhere and at all times obligatory, such as those prescribed in the Decalogue, and the duty of repentance, prayer, &c. And they taught *general principles*, designed to control the conduct in matters respecting which particular precepts could not be given. Thus the learned Grotius makes our Lord say, (see Luke xii. 14,) "Content to give general precepts, which may be very easily applied to all matters by those so disposed, I will not entangle myself with the business of individuals."

Such were the principles stated in the sermon to which I have referred, as showing the limits within which the functions of the ministerial office must be exercised. If any thing could be surprising, in such a day as this, it would be— that principles so manifestly true and Scriptural —principles admitted and asserted by the ablest theological writers for three hundred years, have met with an almost universal condemnation by the religious press. Why, it was only the other day that I saw, in one of our religious papers,

the plain denial that any line can be drawn between the *secular* and the *spiritual*. Well, if
Christian ministers hold an office without metes
and bounds, they may preach on all subjects, and
ought to understand them all. But the idea is
absurd. No civil government could exist, if the
functions of the different offices were not defined
and limited. The ministerial office exerts on the
interests of men a wider influence than any other;
and as, within its legitimate sphere, it is an inestimable blessing, so when perverted, it is fearfully mischievous.

The time is at hand when this great question
respecting the limits within which the functions of
the ministerial office are to be exercised, must be
earnestly discussed. For, it is admitted, that to a
very great extent the proper work of the ministry
is neglected, whilst those clothed with the sacred
office have travelled beyond the limits of their
commission in search of exciting and popular
topics; and the prevailing excitement will render
it extremely difficult to arrest the downward progress of the pulpit.

But another state of things, not referred to in
the discourse of Dr. Hawes, has arisen within the
last three years. The demand is made upon ministers of the Gospel, not to instruct their people

in the truths of God's word, not well understood,
not to inculcate some important precept of the
Gospel demanded by the state of the community,
not to hold forth some precious promise, not to
oppose some error or vice becoming prevalent,
but to define their position respecting some exciting question of the day—a question, it may be,
the examination of which falls not within the
sphere of their studies. But the public have
become excited; and the minister must define
his position. It is not enough that he is chargeable with no word or act to which exception can
be taken. It is not enough that, like Paul, he
does not shun to declare the whole counsel of
God. His private opinions on the exciting topic
must be brought out; and it must be known
whether his *sympathies* are all right. The feelings of his heart in the matter must be brought
out. Now so far as my reading goes, there is
scarcely any thing in the history of despotism,
that can equal this popular tyranny. The Inqui-
sition of Rome has never carried matters so far.
Yet we boast of our free country! Where will
this thing stop?

What are the consequences? The minister
yields to the clamor, and declares his position.
Now, since, in the nature of the case, there must

be differences of opinion about such questions, the
preacher's deliverance gives offence to some of
his people. Then begin debates, and strifes, and
divisions. When I entered the ministry, the
Presbyterian church was *one* noble body. It is
now divided into *five*, and there is reason to fear
further divisions. Other churches have passed
through a similar experience. Where is this
thing to terminate? I do not hesitate to express
the conviction, that unless churches and ministers
can be aroused to see the danger, that in less than
five years their liberties will be gone. Every
time you yield to the clamor, you but increase its
boldness. Admit, that ministers may be called
out in this way, and the day is at hand when
mobs will dictate the doctrines you shall hear, and
the prayers that shall be offered in the churches.
"It was much to the honor of Christ and his doctrines," says the excellent Matthew Henry, in his
commentary on my text, "that he did not inter-
pose as a judge or a divider in matters of this
nature, but left them as he found them, for his
kingdom is not of this world; and in this he hath
given an example to his ministers who deal in
sacred things, not to meddle in disputes about
things secular, not to wade far into controversies
relating to them, but leave that to those whose

proper business it is. Ministers that would mind
their business, and please their Master, must not
entangle themselves with the affairs of this life ;
they forfeit the guidance of God's Spirit, and the
convoy of his providence, when they go out of
their way."

II. We owe it to God and our country, to discharge, each, his own duties without interference
with others. Society, as organized, has its several departments ; and different classes of men are
appointed to attend to its interests. Paul com-
pares the Church to the human body, every member of which has its proper function, and each
ministers to the advantage of all. The illustration
applies almost with equal force to society, as it is
organized. It has its men of business, its civil
and its military officers, its lawyers, doctors, and
ministers ; and its interests are best cared for,
when each attends to his own duties. Physicians are often excessively annoyed by ignorant
nurses and others, whose advice is tendered free
of charge. If the General commanding at York-
town should run off to Washington to look after
the tax bill, or to see that the President does not
err in his duties, the whole country would de-
nounce him. We expect him to attend to the

work which he understands, and which is entrust-
ed to him.   Let others do the same, not excepting
editors, who are presumed to know almost every
thing, but who are as poorly qualified to teach
ministers how to preach and pray, as to direct
generals how to plan their campaigns and fight
their battles.

Christian ministers have their proper place and
work ; and surely their work is sufficient to tax
the wisdom and energies of an angel.   " Who is
sufficient for these things ? "   Where is the faithful minister, who does not often tremble in view
of his failure to meet his responsibilities as he
should ?

III.   We owe it to God and our country, to sustain our Government in the exercise of its *constitutional* functions, and in the discharge of its
legitimate duties.   The interests of the Church are
wrapped up in the destiny of the country, and so
is all else that is dear to us.   Moreover, God
commands us to do this.   " Let every soul be
subject to the higher powers.   For there is no
power but of God : the powers that be are ordain-
ed of God.   Whosoever, therefore, resisteth the
power, resisteth the ordinance of God ; and they
that resist shall receive to themselves damna-

tion." It is not enough that we do not violate the Constitution and laws; we must uphold them. " For this cause pay ye tribute also ; for they are God's ministers attending continually upon this very thing. Render therefore to all their dues; tribute to whom tribute, custom to whom custom, fear to whom fear, honor to whom honor."

The obligation to sustain the Government is even stronger, in a country where the people choose their own rulers; for if they select wise and upright officers, they can have no reason for failing to support them ; and if they choose unwise or wicked rulers, the fault is their own.

This general statement, however, requires these two qualifications : 1st. There is no obligation to *approve* the acts of Government. The right of private judgment is sacred. We may believe and say, that they have acted unwisely or wrongly. The ancient prophets often reproved kings, and exhorted them to repentance, though with purely secular matters they did not interfere. We cannot concede to civil rulers what we deny to the Church of Christ—infallibility. 2d. Even disobedience becomes a duty, whenever civil rulers so far forget themselves, as to command what God has forbidden, or to forbid what He has commanded. Daniel, though a law-abiding man, rebelled against the decree of the king forbidding him to pray ; and when the apostles were forbidden to preach the Gospel, they answered : " Whether it be right in the sight of God, to hearken unto you more than unto God, judge ye." But with these qualifications, subjection to the powers that be, is part of our religion. We must submit, or go elsewhere.

I have now something further to say respecting the charge of sympathizing with secession.

1. It would be strange, indeed, if my sympathies lay in that direction, when for twenty-five years I have stood in public antagonism to the leading doctrine on which the Southern Confederacy is based, viz. : slavery as a desirable institution, and one to be perpetuated. In 1835, the synod of Kentucky, of which I was then a member, after mature deliberation, devised and recommended to their churches a plan for the gradual emancipation of their slaves, and published an address strongly setting forth the evils of slavery, and the duty to seek its removal from amongst us. The plan was adopted by some of the members of my church ; and I defended it in a paper I soon after edited. In 1845, the General Assembly adopted a paper on the subject of slavery, drafted by myself, which terminated the con-

troversy in that body; and in defending the position of our Church on this subject in two lectures published at that time, I used the following language : "The question is not whether there are evils connected with slavery, or whether slavery is itself a great evil—I have not a word to say in favor of slavery as a desirable institution. I have ever deplored its introduction into our country, and would do as much to remove it as any abolitionist, so far as it can be removed by the operation of correct principles. * * * I oppose modern abolitionism, not because it tends to abolish slavery, but because its doctrines are false, and, as carried out in practice, tend to perpetuate slavery, and to aggravate all its evils." By the way, this view is by no means peculiar to me. Rev. Dr. Spring, in his book on the Obligations of the World to the Bible, expresses the same opinion, and says : "The late Dr. Griffin, one of the most devoted friends of the colored race in this land, said to me, a few months before his death—*I do not see that the efforts in favor of immediate emancipation have effected any thing but to rivet the chains of the poor slave.*" Dr. Chalmers strongly expressed the same opinion; and so did the late Dr. Archibald Alexander.

In 1847, a convention was called for the revision of the Constitution of Kentucky; and the question was earnestly discussed, whether provision should be made in the new Constitution for the gradual emancipation of the slaves. Some of the leading Presbyterian ministers in the State publicly advocated the introduction of such a provision. I was then pastor of a church in Cincinnati, and a report being circulated that I was opposed to the emancipation clause, I wrote a letter to a friend who desired to correct this false report, which I will read:

CINCINNATI, June 17th, 1849.

DEAR SIR: Your favor of the 28th ult. came duly to hand. I am surprised that any one should quote or refer to any thing I have said or written, in justification of "anti-emancipation views." Since I first had occasion to investigate the subject of slavery, in its various bearings, my views concerning it have not undergone any material change. Whilst editing the Western Protestant, and the Protestant and Herald in Bardstown, I had occasion repeatedly to express my views of slavery, and I have frequently published and expressed the same views since.

I distinctly deny the fundamental principle of abolitionism, that slaveholding is *in itself* sinful. I hold that there have been and are circumstances which justify individuals in sustaining the relation of masters, or in being slaveholders. I hold, on the other hand, as firmly, that slavery is a complicated evil of immense magnitude, the entire removal of which from our country, should be earnestly and perseveringly sought by all lawful and proper means. It is an evil to the slave, to the master and his family, and to the State.

I need not attempt to point out the many and great evils which flow from the institution of slavery. The work, I rejoice to know, is being done by men better qualified than I to do the subject justice.

Whilst a resident of my native State (and I glory in being a Kentuckian), I watched with intense interest the progress of public sentiment, which was then perceptible, in favor of emancipation and colonization, and I deeply deplored the retrograde movement caused by the abolition excitement. I rejoiced when recently it was proposed to hold a convention for the purpose of remodelling the Constitution, chiefly because I hoped the day had come when Kentucky would take decided measures to rid herself of the evil of slavery. There doubtless are other points in the Constitution, which require change; but if something be not done, and done decidedly, with a view to gradual emancipation, I shall feel painfully convinced that the great work, required alike by the principles of true philanthropy, and by an enlightened regard for the true and permanent interests of the State, has been left undone.

I am convinced that the day must come, and come soon, when Kentucky will move decidedly in the work of emancipation. The tide of public sentiment, if I mistake not, is strongly setting in that direction. The pro-slavery doctrine of some ultra men in the South, can never be generally received in Kentucky. The evils of slavery are too manifest, and the agitation of the question is not now, as too generally heretofore, by fanatical men in the free States. Many of the leading minds of Kentucky, and amongst them many slave-holders, are fully aroused to the importance and the duty of delivering the State from the blight of slavery, and I am persuaded they will not rest till the work is done As it is vain to attempt to satisfy reflecting men that slavery is not an evil, so it is equally vain to say that, though it is an evil, no efforts should be made to remove it. Neither of these propositions can be successfully maintained.

After what I have said, I need not assure you, that I feel a deep interest in the discussion now progressing in Kentucky, and that I rejoice in any measure of success secured by the friends of emancipation and colonization. I should not have remained silent thus long, had I not felt satisfied that the work is in abler hands, and that it is better to leave it to be done chiefly by the citizens of the State. Were I now in Kentucky, where I spent most of my life, I would esteem it no ordinary privilege to stand by the side of those who are so nobly contending for enlightened philanthropy and true policy—who are seeking at once to elevate the colored man, and to promote the best interests of the State.

Having learned, through your kindness, that my views are misrepresented, I deem it a duty alike to myself and the cause which is dear to my heart, to state them distinctly. I should rejoice exceedingly to find my numerous friends in Kentucky all engaged in the present crisis, on the side of emancipation and colonization.   Truly yours,

N. L. RICE.

Such were then my views of the evil of slavery, and of the duty and the interest of my native State with reference to it. Whilst I have never taken any part in political contests, yet, when the question was thrown before the people as to what the State was morally bound to do, I felt free to exert whatever influence I had.

In 1855, when I had the honor of being the Moderator of the General Assembly, the subject of slavery was introduced by the delegates from the several Congregational bodies of New England. On my return home (in St. Louis), I addressed to them ten letters on the subject, from which I will read one or two extracts. Speaking of the reaction in the slaveholding States against emancipation, I said :

This retrograde step has been taken, notwithstanding the earnest efforts of Presbyterians and others to secure a different result. In Missouri, the reaction is equally complete, and, of course, in the more southern States. This is not all, nor the worst. A state of feeling between the North and the South has been produced, which threatens the most disastrous results to our civil Union ; and a dissolution of the Union would not only prove a curse to our country, but to the cause of freedom and of Christianity throughout the world.

In closing these letters, I said :

The time has come, in my humble judgment, when

it is both the interest and the duty of every true Christian and philanthropist to throw the full weight of his influence against the fanaticism of *abolitionism*, and the fanaticism of *pro-slaveryism*. The former is like a quack doctor, who, in his unskilful treatment of a chronic disease, produces other diseases, and threatens to kill the patient; and the latter, like a deranged man, would resist the most skilful physician, and bless God for his malady. They are two extreme errors, each enlisting in its defence the worst passions of human nature, and threatening ruin to Church and State.

In the summer of 1855, the President of the University of Missouri, Rev. Mr. Shannon, manifested great zeal in proving that the Bible and nature *sanction* slavery, and insisted with great earnestness that this doctrine only could save our civil Union. In reviewing one of his publications, in the *St. Louis Presbyterian*, of which I was then the editor, I said, amongst other things:

" 1st. That if what he says is true, there is no hope for the Union. Intelligent men in the free States can be convinced that they ought not to interfere with slavery as it exists amongst us; but you might as well try to convince them that the sun rises in the West, as that the Bible and nature approve of it as a desirable institution. Indeed, it would require more powerful logic than the President can command to satisfy multitudes

in the slaveholding States of the truth of his
views.

"2. The truth is, it is just the extremes to
which men of Mr. Shannon's temperament run,
that endanger the Union. They do more to promote Abolitionism than its advocates can do.
Their doctrines are palpably indefensible, and
their bitter denunciations extremely irritating.
* * * This is not the day for placing such
men in the lead. We need calm, reflecting, judicious men ; and such men rarely take extreme
positions. We have ever firmly opposed abolitionism ; but there is a fanatical pro-slaveryism
which is quite as bad. * * * Certainly, pru-
dent parents will object to placing their sons in
an institution whose President keeps up a con-
stant angry excitement about him, and is found
vociferating in excited political meetings. We
know no other President who has thought it
proper to pursue such a course. Young men
brought under such an influence must be seri-
ously injured. We deeply regret his course, as
adapted to injure the young men intrusted to his
care, to cripple the important institution over
which he presides, and to increase the excited
feelings on the subject of slavery, which all pru-
dent men desire to allay. And since (as he says)

Missouri is *too poor* to buy him off from his indiscretions, it might be well for him to know that she is *rich* enough to dispense with his services."

In the winter of 1860, certain political editors thought it to their interest to assail and misrepresent me and also the Presbyterian Church on the subject of slavery. I regarded it as my duty to correct these slanders, and therefore delivered in my church in Chicago three discourses, which were published and widely circulated. In the first of these discourses, I stated my position, in the following eight particulars:

1. I hold to the *unity* of the human race—that "God hath made of one blood all nations of men for to dwell on all the face of the earth."

2. Consequently I hold that the command—"Thou shalt love thy neighbor as thyself"—applies, in its full force, to every human being. The golden rule—"Whatsoever ye would that men should do to you, do ye even the same unto them"—applies as fully to the Africans as to any other people. The curse pronounced upon Ham does not justify us in enslaving his descendants. I would not buy or hold a man as a slave, unless the circumstances were such that I would justify him in buying and holding me, if our relative positions were changed. I would no sooner maltreat a slave or wound his feelings, than I would do the same thing to his master.

3. I do not hold, therefore, that slavery is a Divine

3

institution, as is marriage, or the parental relation, or as is civil government; nor do I hold that the Bible *sanctions* slavery. To make the broad statement—that it sanctions slavery—would be to say, that it authorizes the strong to enslave the weak, whenever they are so disposed; and it might be construed to justify the abominable slave trade.

4. I distinctly deny the right of any man to traffic in human beings for gain, whether that traffic be the foreign or domestic slave trade. Men who engage in this inhuman business are monsters.

5. I deny the right of any man to separate husbands and wives, parents and children, for his convenience, or for gain. The marriage of slaves, whether recognized by the civil law or not, is as valid in God's law as that of their masters; and what "God hath joined together, let not man put asunder."

6. I deny the right of any man to withhold from his slaves a fair compensation for their labor. Every master, remembering that his Master is in heaven, with whom there is no "respect of persons," is bound to give them that which is "just and equal," taking into account, of course, his obligation to provide for them for life. What the services of any slave are worth, depends, as in the case of other men, on circumstances.

7. I hold it to be the duty of masters not only to give their slaves all needed food, clothing, and shelter, and to treat them kindly, but to afford them the opportunity to receive religious instruction, and to read the word of God. Christ said: "Search the Scriptures;" and no legislature has the right to forbid any man to do it.

8. I hold it to be the duty of those concerned with slavery to elevate their slaves and prepare them for freedom, whenever Divine Providence shall open the way for them to enjoy it.

The Rev. Dr. Hodge, of Princeton, commenting on Col. 4 : 1 and Eph. 6 : 9, says : " Paul requires for slaves not only what is strictly just, but *equality*. This is not only its signification, but its meaning. Slaves are to be treated by their masters on the principles of equality. Not that they are to be equal with their masters in authority, or station, or circumstances; but they are to be treated as having, as men, as husbands, and as parents, equal rights with their masters. It is just as great a sin to deprive a slave of the just recompense for his labor, or to keep him in ignorance, or to take from him his wife or child, as it is to act thus towards a free man.* This is the equality which the law of God demands, and on this principle the final judgment is to be administered. Christ will punish the master for defrauding the slave, as severely as he will punish the slave for robbing his master. The same penalty will be inflicted for the violation of the conjugal or parental rights of the one as of the other. For the Apostle adds, there is no respect of persons with him. * * * Paul carries this so far as to apply the principle not only to the acts, but to the temper of masters. They are not only to act towards

---

* The late beloved and lamented pastor of this church, Dr. Jas. W. Alexander, held, on the subject of slavery, the same views I have ever advocated. In a letter to Dr. Hall, dated New York, June 10th, 1856, referring to the threatening aspect of public affairs, and quoting this language of Dr. Hodge, he says, " How nobly this clear enunciation of a scriptural principle towers above all the extravagancies of both sides."

their slaves on the principles of justice and equity, but
are *to avoid threatening.* This includes all manifesta-
tions of contempt and ill-temper or undue severity.
* * * It is thus that the Holy Spirit deals with slavery." Dr. Hodge well remarks, that the result of
compliance with the Divine precepts, "if it could become general, would be, that first the evils of slavery,
and then slavery itself, would pass away as naturally
and as peacefully as children cease to be minors."

Holding these views, I also hold that slavery, as it
exists in our country, originated in violence and wickedness. I regard it as always an evil to both parties; and
I do firmly believe, that the effects of the prevalence of
the Gospel will be gradually to abate its evils, and
ultimately to remove it from the country. I need
scarcely say, that I cannot defend or justify much of the
legislation of the slaveholding States on this subject;
and that I would hold no Christian fellowship with any
man or Church, who would refuse to be governed in
the treatment of their slaves by the law of God, instead
of the existing civil code.

Thus you have my record during a period of
more than a quarter of a century ; a record made
partly whilst I labored in slaveholding States,
partly whilst laboring in the free States. In both
I have publicly advocated gradual emancipation
and colonization, in order to remove what I have
ever affirmed to be an evil of terrible magnitude.
In both I have uniformly and with equal earnestness opposed abolitionism and pro-slaveryism. I

have published on this general subject, in its different phases, what would fill two or three volumes; and I would not to-day, if I could, change a single sentiment I have published, but would rejoice to spread every line before the public now. For nearly thirty years I have publicly defended the position of our Church, as defined by the General Assembly of 1818 ; and once and again the General Assembly has endorsed the paper on this subject, which was drafted by myself, and adopted almost unanimously by the Assembly of 1845.

Now, I leave all honest and candid men to judge, how far one holding such views could sympathize with secession.

Meanwhile, no one acquainted with human nature will be surprised that, standing as I have ever stood, in opposition to the two extreme opinions on the subject of slavery, I have been charged by partisans on either side with being decidedly *pro-slavery* and decidedly *abolitionist* in my views. Less than three years ago, both these charges were made against me at the same time by prominent ministers, (N. School,) in the North and in the South. The *New York Evangelist*, which has chosen recently to say some offensive things about my views, did me the honor to represent

me as defending slavery " with the gallant bear-
ing of an old chevalier, careless of all odds ; "
and, at the same time, Rev. Messrs. Newton and
McClean, of Mississippi, held me up to the public
in a political paper, as a decided Abolitionist. A
friend, writing to me, said : " They insinuate that
you and Dr. R. J. Breckinridge are in the
abolition list ; that you teach that slavery is an
evil of immense magnitude ; that you were the
chairman of the committee that drew up the report on slavery in 1845, and said, that there is
not one expression in the paper adopted in '45
that wears a pro-slavery appearance, or that will
bear any such interpretation, &c. ; and refer to
your editorials in the *St. Louis Presbyterian*
of 1856–'57." Now, what confidence can be
placed in the statements of men so blinded by
prejudice that, looking at the same object, one
pronounces it white as snow, the other, black as
night ?

2. Now, with regard to secession itself, it so
happens that my position was taken, and my
views published more than fifteen months ago, before the war began. I have never been accustomed
to wait till the last moment, to take my position
on any questions on which duty may require me
to speak ; and my worst enemies, I believe, have

never charged me with occupying an ambiguous position on any such subject.

The rupture which has taken place, and the terrible war now desolating our noble country, did not take me by surprise. For years past, standing in a position to survey the whole ground, and to observe the workings of moral principles and of passions, I saw the increasing danger, though sometimes more hopeful, sometimes in despair. Over and over, for twenty years past, I have given warning, as far as I could make my voice heard and my pen known, that this terrible storm was approaching; and as often have I exhorted conservative men on both sides of the line to awake to the danger and exert themselves to avert it. Some ridiculed, and others disbelieved. And one of the most amazing facts in history is the fact, that this catastrophe took intelligent men and Christian ministers at the North, as well as many in the South, by surprise. In my lectures on slavery, in 1845, I said : " This subject is now exciting very general interest among all classes of people in our country, is occasioning division in the Church of Christ, *and even threatening the destruction of our civil Union.* Already, it has divided the Methodist and Baptist churches ; and it is now agitating to the very centre the N.

School Presbyterian Church; whilst fanatical Abolitionists are denouncing our civil Union as most iniquitous, and not to be tolerated. At such a time, it behooves every man to inform himself fully on the whole subject, that his influence may be thrown where it should be. At such a time it becomes the duty of those who deprecate such divisions and agitations to contribute as they can to the dissemination of correct principles. * * * The Abolitionists will never abolish slavery, nor improve the condition of the slaves; but if their principles could prevail to any great extent, they would not only abolish the peace, harmony, and union of the churches of Christ, but the Christian ministry, the Sabbath, (which Gerrit Smith and others have devoted to political harangues,) and our civil Union. *It would involve our happy country in a most dreadful civil war.* * * * Finally, if slavery is ever to cease in America, it must be abolished by the people of the slaveholding States, or with their approbation; and the necessary change in public sentiment must be wrought, as it has been elsewhere, by the influence of the Gospel of Christ, not by Abolitionist societies; not by denouncing and excommunicating slaveholders, simply because they are such;

not by the mad and wicked attempt to destroy our civil Union."

In June, 1856, in an article in the *St. Louis Presbyterian*, I remarked as follows : " The day has come, when wise and good men are compelled to doubt the permanency of our civil Union, *and should it be dissolved, both North and South will be ruined*, not simply because of the dissolution, but because it will be followed by fearful civil commotions, destroying our prosperity, and exposing us to the aggression of foreign enemies, and because the state of morals which will produce dissolution, will continue in other ways to do the work of destruction. A more glorious heritage God never gave to any nation than he has given to ours ; and greater folly was never known than that which now threatens to turn the blessing into a fearful curse."

I wish I could, without wearying you, read the entire article. I would gladly lay before you the many articles I have published on this fearful subject ; for, whilst I claim no extraordinary wisdom, you would see that I foresaw and pointed out the very course things have taken.

But when, nearly eighteen months ago, it became clear to all, that our noble Union must, for the time, be dissolved, editing a paper in Chicago

which had some circulation in the South, I at
once gave my views of the great wrong about to
be perpetrated. In a correspondence with one of
the Presbyterian ministers of Georgia, published
in the *Presbyterian Expositor*, my position was
distinctly defined.

I did not say that the South had no grievances,
and that the North is infallible. Neither of these
things, in my opinion, is true. There can be no
greater folly than to claim *sectional infallibility*,
in a quarrel which has been waxing more and
more violent for a quarter of a century.

Nor did I undertake to express an opinion
respecting the constitutional questions so prominent in the controversy; whether the Constitution,
rightly interpreted, protects slavery in the Terri-
tories or not; or whether it allows particular
States to withdraw from the civil compact. I
make no pretensions to skill in expounding civil
constitutions. The studies of my life have lain in
other directions. Moreover, as I have heretofore
said, I deny the right of any minister of Christ,
whatever his knowledge of law, to give forth, as
a minister, any opinions on such subjects. As individuals and as citizens, ministers have the right
to form and hold their own opinions on all subjects, but when they speak or write as ministers

of Christ, they must deliver to men *his message*, not their political notions. What right have they to say, *in the name of Christ*, what is the meaning of the Constitution on such subjects? Has he given them any such message? Moreover, it is impossible for ministers of Christ to involve themselves in such controversies, without crippling their ministerial influence, and disturbing the peace of the Church. These things I dare not do. I am charged with interests that rise infinitely higher than those of the State; and I know I never serve my country so well, as when I oppose with the power of the Gospel the corruption that is ruining it. And why should I undertake to enlighten the people on such subjects, when there are all around me laymen, whose business it is to study such questions, who are incomparably better qualified to discuss them? If ministers of the Gospel are to take sides in such discussions, then let them first go through a course of legal reading and study. Have they time? If not, let them preach what they understand.

But apart altogether from the constitutional questions involved, there are *moral* grounds on which I pronounced the disruption of our civil union a great wrong. They are the following:

1. The South had had its fair share in pro-

ducing the alienation which existed, and had, in ways which I pointed out, driven from them multitudes who desired to stand by them. They, therefore, could not of right take advantage of their own wrong to bring upon the country so fearful a catastrophe.

2. There had been no fair issue made before the people to test the question, whether the majority of the Northern people were disposed to trample upon their rights. Instead of sending forth one candidate representing what they wanted, they had sent forth three—thus insuring their own defeat, and leaving the question undecided, how far the people were disposed to do them justice. And I expressed strongly the opinion, that the majority of the Northern people were not disposed to interfere with any of their constitutional rights. Now, whatever right of revolution may exist, in case of great oppression ; or whatever right may exist in the States to secede in case of a clearly expressed purpose of a majority of the States to trample under foot important provisions of the Constitution ; it is a clear moral principle, that no such right can exist, until a fair issue has been made, and it has become clear, that the minority are to be denied rights essential to their well-being.

On such grounds as these, I declared my un-doubting conviction, that the movement in the South was a great and terrible wrong. The publication of these views, in connection with my views of slavery, called forth decided expressions of condemnation in all the Southern papers that I read. If my sympathies were with secession, they utterly failed to discover it, and thought they discovered the opposite. They thought my language too severe also in my review of Dr. Palmer's celebrated sermon. I thank God, that my opinions on this subject were given to the public, before the war commenced; and when it is remembered that I was, at that time, the pastor of a church, the large majority of whose male members belong to the political party now in power; and that with entire unanimity and great earnestness they sought to retain me as their pastor, after the publication of my opinions; you can judge how far I manifested sympathy with secession.

Now, as to the war, I have a few things to say. I have said, we owe it to God and our country, each, to discharge his duty in his own sphere. We have a government upon whom is devolved the duty and the responsibility of determining whether, in case of disagreement between different sections of the country, such measures can be adopted and such compromises made, consistently with the honor and the interests of the country, as may avert the horrors of civil war. Upon them is devolved the solemn and responsible duty of deciding when war has become inevitable— when duty and interests require the country to engage in the fearful work. In seeking and accepting the offices they fill, they expressed their readiness to assume the responsibility ; and, so far as I know, they have shown no disposition to shrink from it. They did not ask the opinion of ministers of the Gospel. Now, so long as peace was possible, I labored with others, publicly and privately, to make peace. When those upon whom the responsibility rests, declared war necessary and inevitable, I regarded it as my duty to acquiesce, and to teach others to acquiesce, and to sustain the Government.

But my responsibilities are sufficiently great, without assuming those which properly rest upon others. I think, I could explain those principles of God's word, which ought to control civil governments in determining whether it is right to go to war ; but it belongs to *citizens*, and especially to *statesmen*, to make the application of those principles to the facts in the case. For my right hand, I would not *volunteer* to decide such a question, when God has not required it. When it has been decided by the constitutional authorities, my duty as a minister is to teach my people, if they require to be taught, to be subject to the powers that be, to sustain the government under which they live. If it were the duty of ministers to pronounce upon the wisdom or righteousness of every war in which their country may be involved, then they would be constantly liable to be obliged to take public ground against their government; for unwise and unrighteous wars are common in our world. But no government could exist were individuals and ministers should be allowed to decide upon the policy to be pursued, or to make opposition to a war decided upon, as a political necessity.

Yet I do greatly mourn over the necessity of such a war. I mourn over the desolation of our noble country. I mourn over the untimely death of multitudes of the young men of the country. I mourn over the stricken families, the widows and orphans, in every part of the land. I mourn over the torn, divided, distracted Church, bought with a Saviour's blood, and which I love above my chief joy. I mourn over the disgrace inflicted upon religion, the abounding of wickedness, the interruption of the Church in the noble work of evangelizing the world. But, with a sad and bleeding heart, I must sustain my government, and pray that God, in infinite mercy, will turn away from the fierceness of His just displeasure, and so guide our rulers, and so dispose the hearts of men in every part of the land, and so order events, that we may soon see our country again united in peace under its noble Constitution.

IV. We owe it to God and our country to tell our rulers and the people, that war, especially civil war, is a Divine judgment upon the nation for its sins; and that only repentance and reformation can give the Scriptural and rational hope of such a peace as we desire; that our dependence must be on God, not on the skill of our officers, the training of our soldiers, and the abundance of our resources. It is cruel unfaithfulness for Christian ministers to declaim with politicians, and predict victory and triumph, without insisting upon the necessity of repentance and reformation.

In 1690, that great and good man, Archbishop Tillotson, preached a *Fast-sermon on war*, and his text was Ecclesiastes ix. 11: "I returned and saw under the sun, that the race is not to the swift, nor the battle to the strong." The whole

discourse, rich with scripture truth, delivered with
the spirit becoming an ambassador of Christ, is
designed to show the danger in war of trusting
in any thing but the Lord of Hosts. Soon after,
he preached another sermon before the Lord
Mayor of London from the text, " Be thou instructed, O Jerusalem, lest my soul depart from
thee, lest I make thee desolate, a land not inhab-
ited ; " Jer. vi. 8. The title of the sermon is
" *The Ruin of a Sinful People.*" It is, as the
text and title import, a solemn appeal and warning on the absolute necessity of repentance and
reformation, in order to success in war. In 1691
he preached another sermon—a Fast-sermon, before the queen, of a similar character. Dr. Doddridge, author of the Paraphrase of the New Testa-
ment, preached, on a day of public humiliation, in
time of war, on Deut. xxiii. 9, " When thou goest
forth against thine enemies, then keep thee from
every wicked thing." This excellent discourse is
of the same character, and breathes the same
spirit as those already mentioned. He states and
illustrates the following doctrine : " I think I
may very safely venture to affirm, that we can
never form any just expectation of continued success in our military affairs, unless there be a zeal-
ous concern about a reformation in our morals,

and unless national piety and virtue be our earnest, governing care." On a similar occasion, Dr. Witherspoon preached a sermon in Scotland, a hundred years ago, of precisely the same character. The title sufficiently indicates its character, viz. : "*Prayer for National Prosperity, and for the Revival of Religion, inseparably connected.*"

Such was the character of the discourses which great and good men of other days felt it their duty to preach, in times of war, to both rulers and people. I would not look too darkly at our affairs, but the most of the discourses I have read on the present war, stand in alarming contrast with those. I cannot help dreading the consequences. We have seen our noble army hurled headlong into battle, with a thousand prophecies of certain victory ; and we have seen them flying in disorder and terror from the field, leaving the slain scattered over the ground by hundreds. Such events might never have occurred, if our rulers and the people had been faithfully warned, instead of being excited by glowing predictions. Some of you may not have forgotten, that my morning sermon, on the second Sabbath of my labors amongst you, when the city was in a blaze of excitement, was on the text,

L. of C.

"The Lord reigneth ; let the people tremble."
In that discourse I tried to set forth the great
Scripture truths so necessary to be known and
felt, yet so likely to be forgotten at such a time.

V. We owe it to God and our country, to
maintain during the war such a temper and spirit
as is not offensive to Him, and as may afford
ground of hope, that when peace returns, it may
be permanent. The tendency of war is to excite
the worst feelings of the human heart, and to produce permanent alienations. This is preëminently
true of *civil war*. The faithful 'minister must
warn his people on this point ; for it is offensive
to God to go to war with vindictive feelings. "Too
keen a resentment," said Doddridge, in the discourse already mentioned, "for the injuries received from our enemies, growing into a malig-
nant hatred against them, is another evil, which we
should be particularly solicitous to avoid." England was then engaged in a war with Spain, and
had had great provocations. Still, in the true
spirit of a minister of peace, Doddridge gave
this warning, and added : "War, in such circumstances as ours, is the rigorous and severe work
of justice, and must be done ; but, methinks, a
humane heart consents to it with some sensible

regret, and will sometimes bleed to think, that those benevolent and brotherly cares, that ought to fill the heart of one man for another, and of one nation for another, should be turned into thoughts and schemes of destruction, and give place to contrivances how men may be slaughtered, and cities laid waste, and the beauties of nature and art ravaged and defaced."

How much more necessary is it to guard our tempers and spirits, when *civil* war rages, and especially when the mournful sight is witnessed of Christian men, children of the same Father, heirs of the same heavenly inheritance, who in days past have communed at the same sacred table, met in hostile array to aim at each others' bosoms the deadly blow. In the South are tens of thousands of men and women whose piety we cannot question, many whom we have known and loved, as the faithful children of God. I think they have been most sadly misled, or carried by the resistless tide of passion raging around them; but their true piety I cannot doubt. And the Holy Spirit has formed a tie between us and them, which the conflicts brought on the country by bad or deceived men, ought not to sunder— ties that are to endure, when all earthly ties are forever sundered. If we are commanded to love our worst enemies, much more are we bound still to love those children of our Heavenly Father, who are in no sense our personal enemies; and to guard against vindictive feelings towards even those who make no professions of piety.

I, therefore, have no sympathy with much that I hear and read in addresses and sermons, that seems adapted only to intensify amongst the people of the North feelings naturally too strong; and, if read in the South, would only increase that hatred which will yet prove the greatest obstacle to a reconstruction of the Union. We are not appointed of God to punish the sins of our fellow-men. He says: " Vengeance is mine." Let us not dare to step into his place, and assume his prerogatives. When war becomes necessary, it is a dreadful necessity, over which every Christian heart must mourn. And the blessing of God cannot rest upon those who increase its horrors by awakening and stirring up vindictive feelings. They who march to battle, and those who desire their success, should alike put away from them this wicked feeling.

At the close of this war, if it prove successful on our part, we are to try an experiment, which, so far as my reading extends, has never been tried in this world, viz.: *to maintain a free government*

*over an immense territory, whose interests, as to
the different sections, differ widely, with the moral
forces all antagonistic along a line running
through the middle of it.* So far as I know, the
experiment has never been made. Whether we
shall make it successfully, must depend, to a great
extent, upon the question, whether ministers of
the Gospel shall be willing, and shall be allowed,
to confine themselves to their appropriate work.
I think it cannot be doubted, that the chief perils
of this nation will be encountered *at the end of,
the war.* Then the common danger, which now
produces general union, will disappear ; and new
and most difficult questions must be settled, which
will test to the utmost our moral principles and
the wisdom of our statesmen. The danger that is
now upon us took ministers, statesmen, and people by surprise. The next and greater peril will,
in all likelihood, overtake them in the same way.
O ! that men would consider in time, to avert
other and greater catastrophes.

I will close what I have to say with the closing
sentiment of one of my discourses, delivered in
Chicago, on slavery.

You know, my friends, that I might gain popularity
by falling in with the current that has set in so strongly
in this latitude, and raising the Abolitionist (war) shout.

But I see before me an august tribunal, which I am hourly approaching ; and I see around me the raging of fierce passions, threatening the ruin of Church and State. God helping me, I never will yield to popular clamor at the expense of His truth, and of the interests of His church and of my country. May He subdue passion and guide us into His own pure truth.

www.ingramcontent.com/pod-product-compliance
Lightning Source LLC
Chambersburg PA
CBHW022153090426
42742CB00010B/1492